The Poetry Of Kabir

Kabir, (meaning Great and one of the 99 names of God in Arabic), was a mystic and poet, born around 1440 whose work continues to be revered today by Muslims, Sufis, Sikhs and Hindus and is the founder of the Kabir Panth ("Path of Kabir"), a religious community mainly in India with approximately 10 million members. He was born in Varanasi to poor Muslim parents, although some say he was the child of a Brahmin widow and said of himself that he was *"at once the child of Allah and Ram."* He grew up learning his father's craft of weaving and very unusually for a Muslim, overcame obstacles to become a disciple of Saint or Swami Ramananda, the leading pioneer of the Bhakti movement, which promoted salvation for all. We cannot be sure of what religious teaching he received in Ramananda's ashram as Ramananda died when Kabir was 13 but we do know that he did not renounce his worldly life, as he married and had children, and was disdainful of professional piety which led to later persecution by religious authorities. This was further amplified by his progressive philosophy of social equality and his spiritual synthesis of Hindu ideas of karma and reincarnation and Muslim beliefs of one god and no idolatry or caste system.

We do know that he had no formal education and remained almost entirely illiterate and expressed his poems as 'bāṇīs' meaning utterances in Hindi although he borrowed from various dialects. His songs and couplets were part of a strong oral tradition in the region and although spread across northern India orally were also written down by two of his disciples, namely Bhāgodās and Dharmadās. Kabir's style was inventive and imaginative and able to capture the attention of a wide range of Indians and provide a path to spiritual awakening which for Kabir was mainly about love and brotherhood and not to be divorced from daily life. *"All our actions performed anywhere are our duties, and work is worship."* His work is understood and accessible to generations of Indians, more so than any other Saint and in India remains one of the most quoted mystic poets of all time. His ability to simplify and use examples of our universal daily life to enhance our spiritual well being and acceptance of our own self make his work very relevant today as is apparent in this volume.

Kabir is thought to have lived an exceptionally long life and probably died in 1518. It is said that his Hindu followers wanted his body cremated and his Muslim followers wanted his body buried and a fight therefore ensued. When they finally lifted the cloth that covered his dead body they found flowers and took half each for his last rites.

Index Of Poems
The Word

Abode Of The Beloved
Are You Looking For Me?
Between The Poles Of The Conscious
Brother, I've Seen Some
The Lord Is In Me
Chewing Slowly
Do Not Go To The Garden Of Flowers
Friend, Hope For The Guest While You Are Alive
The Middle Region Of The Sky
There's A Moon Inside My Body
Friend, Wake Up! Why Do You Go On Sleeping?
Hang Up The Swing Of Love Today!
The Moon Shines In My Body
Having Crossed The River
The River And Its Waves Are One
He's That Rascally Kind Of Yogi
The Self Forgets Itself
Hey Brother, Why Do You Want Me To Talk?
Hiding In This Cage
To Be A Slave Of Intensity
His Death In Benares
The Spiritual Athlete Often Changes The Color Of His Clothes
The Time Before Death
To Thee Thou Hast Drawn My Love
Hope For Him
How Do You
To What Shore Would You Cross
How Humble Is God
The Swan Flies Away
I Burst Into Laughter
What Kind Of God?
I Have Attained The Eternal Bliss
I Have Been Thinking
I Laugh When I Hear That The Fish In The Water Is Thirsty
When He Himself Reveals Himself
I Played Day And Night
I Said To The Wanting-Creature Inside Me
When I Found The Boundless Knowledge
I Talk To My Inner Lover, And I Say, Why Such Rush?
I Won't Come
When The Day Came
Illusion And Reality
It Is Needless To Ask Of A Saint
I've Burned My Own House Down
Knowing Nothing Shuts The Iron Gates
Lamps Burn In Every House
Lift The Veil
Looking At The Grinding Stones - Dohas (Couplets) I
When You Were Born In This world - Dohas II
Where Do You Search Me
Many Hoped
My Body And My mind

My Body Is Flooded
Where Spring, The Lord Of The Seasons
My Swan, Let Us Fly
O Friend
O How May I Ever Express That Secret Word?
O Lord Increate, Who Will Serve Thee?
O My Heart! The Supreme Spirit
O Servant Where Dost Thou Seek Me
O Slave, Liberate Yourself
Oh Friend, I Love You, Think This Over
Plucking Your Eyebrows
Tell Me Brother
Tell Me, O Swan, Your Ancient Tale
Tentacles Of Time
The Bhakti Path
The Bride-Soul
The Dropp And The Sea
The Guest Is Inside You, And Also Inside Me
The Impossible Pass
The Last Flight
The Light Of The Sun
Within This Earthen Vessel

The Word

Find the word, understand the word,
Depend on the word;
The word is heaven and space, the word the earth,
The word the universe.
The word is in our ears, the word is on our tongues,
The word the idol.
The word is the holy book, the word is harmony,
The word is music.
The word is magic, the word the Guru.
The word is the body, the word is the spirit, the word is being,
The word Not-being.
The word is man, the word is woman,
The Worshipped Great.
The word is the seen and unseen, the word is the existent
And the non-existent.
Know the word, says Kabir,
The word is All-powerful.

Abode Of The Beloved

Oh Companion That Abode Is Unmatched,
Where My Complete Beloved Is.

In that Place There Is No Happiness or Unhappiness,
No Truth or Untruth

Neither Sin Nor Virtue.
There Is No Day or Night, No Moon or Sun,
There Is Radiance Without Light.

There Is No Knowledge or Meditation
No Repetition of Mantra or Austerities,
Neither Speech Coming From Vedas or Books.
Doing, Not-Doing, Holding, Leaving
All These Are All Lost Too In This Place.

No Home, No Homeless, Neither Outside or Inside,
Micro and Macrocosm Are Non-Existent.
Five Elemental Constituents and the Trinity Are Both Not There
Witnessing Un-struck Shabad Sound is Also Not There.

No Root or Flower, Neither Branch or Seed,
Without a Tree Fruits are Adorning,
Primordial Om Sound, Breath-Synchronized Soham,
This and That - All Are Absent, The Breath Too Unknown

Where the Beloved Is There is Utterly Nothing
Says Kabir I Have Come To Realize.
Whoever Sees My Indicative Sign
Will Accomplish the Goal of Liberation.

Are You Looking For Me?
Are you looking for me? I am in the next seat.
My shoulder is against yours.
you will not find me in the stupas, not in Indian shrine
rooms, nor in synagogues, nor in cathedrals:
not in masses, nor kirtans, not in legs winding
around your own neck, nor in eating nothing but
vegetables.

When you really look for me, you will see me
instantly
you will find me in the tiniest house of time.

Kabir says: Student, tell me, what is God?
He is the breath inside the breath.

Between The Poles Of The Conscious
Between the poles of the conscious and the unconscious, there has the mind made a swing:
Thereon hang all beings and all worlds, and that swing never ceases its sway.
Millions of beings are there: the sun and the moon in their courses are there:
Millions of ages pass, and the swing goes on.
All swing! the sky and the earth and the air and the water; and the Lord Himself taking form:
And the sight of this has made Kabîr a servant.

Brother, I've Seen Some
Brother, I've seen some
Astonishing sights:
A lion keeping watch
Over pasturing cows;
A mother delivered
After her son was;
A guru prostrated
Before his disciple;
Fish spawning
On treetops;
A cat carrying away
A dog;
A gunny-sack
Driving a bullock-cart;
A buffalo going out to graze,
Sitting on a horse;
A tree with its branches in the earth,
Its roots in the sky;
A tree with flowering roots.

This verse, says Kabir,
Is your key to the universe.
If you can figure it out.

The Lord Is In Me
The Lord is in me, and the Lord is in you,
As life is hidden in every seed.
So rubble your pride, my friend,
And look for Him within you.

When I sit in the heart of His world
A million suns blaze with light,
A burning blue sea spreads across the sky,
Life's turmoil falls quiet,
All the stains of suffering wash away.

Listen to the unstruck bells and drums!
Love is here; plunge into its rapture!
Rains pour down without water;
Rivers are streams of light.

How could I ever express
How blessed I feel
To revel in such vast ecstasy
In my own body?

This is the music
Of soul and soul meeting,

Of the forgetting of all grief.
This is the music
That transcends all coming and going

Chewing Slowly
Chewing slowly,
Only after I'd eaten
My grandmother,
Mother,
Son-in-law,
Two brothers-in-law,
And father-in-law
(His big family included)
In that order,
And had for dessert
The town's inhabitants,

Did I find, says Kabir,
The beloved that I've become
One with.

Do Not Go To The Garden Of Flowers
Do not go to the garden of flowers!
Do not go to the garden of flowers!
O Friend! go not there;
In your body is the garden of flowers.

Take your seat on the thousand petals of the lotus,
and there gaze on the Infinite Beauty.

Friend, Hope For The Guest While You Are Alive
Friend, hope for the Guest while you are alive.
Jump into experience while you are alive!
Think... and think... while you are alive.
What you call 'salvation' belongs to the time
before death.

If you don't break your ropes while you're alive,
do you think
ghosts will do it after?

The idea that the soul will join with the ecstatic
just because the body is rotten—
that is all fantasy.
What is found now is found then.
If you find nothing now,
you will simply end up with an apartment
in the City of Death.
If you make love with the divine now, in the next life
you will have the face of satisfied desire.

So plunge into the truth, find out who the Teacher is,
believe in the Great Sound!

Kabir says this: When the Guest is being search for,
it is the intensity of the longing for the Guest
that does all the work.
Look at me, and you will see a slave of that intensity.

The Middle Region Of The Sky
The middle region of the sky,
wherein the spirit dwelleth,
is radiant with the music of light;

There, where the pure and white music blossoms,
my Lord takes His delight.

In the wondrous effulgence of each hair of His body, t
he brightness of millions of suns and of moons is lost.

On that shore there is a city,
where the rain of nectar pours and pours,
and never ceases.
Kabîr says: 'Come, O Dharmadas!
and see my great Lord's Durbar.'

There's A Moon Inside My Body
The moon shines in my body, but my blind eyes cannot see it:
The moon is within me, and so is the sun.
The unstruck drum of Eternity is sounded within me; but my deaf ears cannot hear it.

So long as man clamours for the I and the Mine, his works are as naught:
When all love of the I and the Mine is dead, then the work of the Lord is done.
For work has no other aim than the getting of knowledge:
When that comes, then work is put away.

The flower blooms for the fruit: when the fruit comes, the flower withers.
The musk is in the deer, but it seeks it not within itself: it wanders in quest of grass.

Friend, Wake Up! Why Do You Go On Sleeping?
Friend, wake up! Why do you go on sleeping?
The night is over— do you want to lose the day
the same way?
Other women who managed to get up early have
already found an elephant or a jewel...
so much was lost already while you slept...
and that was so unnecessary!

The one who loves you understood, but you did not.
You forgot to make a place in your bed next to you.
Instead you spent your life playing.
In your twenties you did not grow
because you did not know who your Lord was.
Wake up! Wake up! There's no one in your bed—
He left you during the long night.

Kabir says: The only woman awake is the woman
who has heard the flute!

Hang Up The Swing Of Love Today!
Hang the body and the mind between the arms of the beloved,
in the ecstasy of love's joy:

Bring the tearful streams of the rainy clouds to your eyes,
and cover your heart with the shadow of darkness:

Bring your face nearer to his ear,
and speak of the deepest longings of your heart.

Kabir says: 'Listen to me brother!
bring the vision of the Beloved in your heart.'

The Moon Shines In My Body
The moon shines in my body,
but my blind eyes cannot see it:
The moon is within me,
and so is the sun.

The unstruck drum of Eternity is sounded within me;
but my deaf ears cannot hear it.

So long as man clamours for the 'I' and the 'Mine',
his works are as naught:
When all love of the 'I' and the 'Mine' is dead,
then the work of the Lord is done.

For work has no other aim than the getting of knowledge:
When that comes, then work is put away.

The flower blooms for the fruit:
when the fruit comes, the flower withers.
The musk is in the deer,
but it seeks it not within itself:
it wanders in quest of grass.

Having Crossed The River

Having crossed the river,
where will you go, O friend?

There's no road to tread,
No traveler ahead,
Neither a beginning, nor an end.

There's no water, no boat, no boatman, no cord;
No earth is there, no sky, no time, no bank, no ford.

You have forgotten the Self within,
Your search in the void will be in vain;
In a moment the life will ebb
And in this body you won't remain.

Be ever conscious of this, O friend,
You've to immerse within your Self;
Kabir says, salvation you won't then need,
For what you are, you would be indeed.

The River And Its Waves Are One
The river and its waves are one
surf: where is the difference between the river and its waves?

When the wave rises,
it is the water;
and when it falls,
it is the same water again.

Tell me, Sir, where is the distinction?
Because it has been named as wave,
shall it no longer be considered as water?

Within the Supreme Brahma,
the worlds are being told like beads:
Look upon that rosary with the eyes of wisdom.

He's That Rascally Kind Of Yogi
He's that rascally kind of yogi
who has no sky or earth,
no hand, foot,
form or shape.
Where there's no market
he sets up shop,
weighs things
and keeps the accounts.
No deeds, no creeds,
no yogic powers,
not even a horn or gourd,
so how can he

go begging?

'I know you
and you know me
and I'm inside of you.'

When there isn't a trace
of creation or destruction,
what do you meditate on?
That yogi built a house
brimful of Ram.
He has no healing herbs,
his root-of-life
is Ram.

He looks and looks
at the juggler's tricks,
the magician's sleight-of-hand -
Kabir says, saints, he's made it
to the King's land.

The Self Forgets Itself
The self forgets itself
as a frantic dog in a glass temple
barks himself to death;
as a lion, seeing a form in the well,
leaps on the image;
as a rutting elephant sticks his tusk
in a crystal boulder.
The monkey has his fistful of sweets
and won't let go. So
from house to house
he gibbers.
Kabir says, parrot-on-a-pole:
who has caught you?

Hey Brother, Why Do You Want Me To Talk?
Hey brother, why do you want me to talk?
Talk and talk and the real things get lost.

Talk and talk and things get out of hand.
Why not stop talking and think?

If you meet someone good, listen a little, speak;
If you meet someone bad, clench up like a fist.

Talking with a wise man is a great reward.
Talking with a fool? A waste.

Kabir says: A pot makes noise if it's half full,
But fill it to the brim - no sound.

Hiding In This Cage
Hiding in this cage
of visible matter

is the invisible
lifebird

pay attention
to her

she is singing
your song

To Be A Slave Of Intensity
Friend, hope for the guest while you are alive.
Jump into experience while you are alive!
Think...and think...while you are alive.
What you call 'salvation' belongs to the time before death.

If you don't break your ropes while you're alive,
do you think
ghosts will do it after?

The idea that the soul will join with the ecstatic
Just because the body is rotten -
that is all fantasy.
What is found now is found then.
If you find nothing now,
you will simply end up with an apartment in the City of Death.
If you make love with the divine now, in the next life you will have the face of satisfied desire.

So plunge into the truth, find out who the Teacher is,
Believe in the Great Sound!

Kabir says this: When the guest is being searched for, it is the intensity of the longing for the Guest that does all the work.
Look at me, and you will see a slave of that intensity.

His Death In Benares
His death in Benares
Won't save the assassin
From certain hell,

Any more than a dip
In the Ganges will send

Frogs—or you—to paradise.

My home, says Kabir,
Is where there's no day, no night,
And no holy book in sight

To squat on our lives.

The Spiritual Athlete Often Changes The Color Of His Clothes
The spiritual athlete often changes the color of his clothes,
and his mind remains gray and loveless.

He sits inside a shrine room all day,
so that the Guest has to go outdoors and praise the rocks.

Or he drills holes in his ears, his hair grows
enormous and matted,
people mistake him for a goat...
He goes out into wilderness areas, strangles his impulses,
and makes himself neither male nor female...

He shaves his skull, puts his robe in an orange vat,
reads the Bhagavad-Gita, and becomes a terrific talker.

Kabir says: Actually you are going in a hearse
to the country of death,
bound hand and foot!

The Time Before Death
Friend? hope for the Guest while you are alive.
Jump into experience while you are alive!
Think... and think... while you are alive.
What you call 'salvation' belongs to the time
before death.

If you don't break your ropes while you're alive,
do you think ghosts will do it after?

The idea that the soul will join with the ecstatic
just because the body is rotten
that is all fantasy.
What is found now is found then.
If you find nothing now,
you will simply end up with an apartment in the
City of Death.
If you make love with the divine now, in the next
life you will have the face of satisfied desire.

So plunge into the truth, find out who the Teacher is,
Believe in the Great Sound!

Kabir says this: When the Guest is being searched for,
it is the intensity of the longing for the Guest
that does all the work.

Look at me, and you will see a slave of that intensity.

To Thee Thou Hast Drawn My Love
To Thee Thou hast drawn my love, O Fakir!
I was sleeping in my own chamber,
and Thou didst awaken me;
striking me with Thy voice, O Fakir!
I was drowning in the deeps of the ocean of this world, and
Thou didst save me: upholding me with Thine arm, O Fakir!
Only one word and no second-
and Thou hast made me tear off all
my bonds, O Fakir!
Kabîr says, 'Thou hast united Thy heart to my heart, O Fakir! '

Hope For Him
O friend! hope for Him whilst you live, know whilst you live,
understand whilst you live: for in life deliverance abides.
If your bonds be not broken whilst living, what hope of
deliverance in death?
It is but an empty dream, that the soul shall have union with Him
because it has passed from the body:
If He is found now, He is found then,
If not, we do but go to dwell in the City of Death.
If you have union now, you shall have it hereafter.
Bathe in the truth, know the true Guru, have faith in the true
Name!
Kabîr says: 'It is the Spirit of the quest which helps; I am the slave of this Spirit
of the quest.

How Do You
How do you,
Asks the chief of police,
Patrol a city
Where the butcher shops
Are guarded by vultures;
Where bulls get pregnant,
Cows are barren,
And calves give milk
Three times a day;
Where mice are boatmen
And tomcats the boats
They row;
Where frogs keep snakes
As watchdogs,

And jackals
Go after lions?

Does anyone know
What I'm talking about?
Says Kabir.

To What Shore Would You Cross
To what shore would you cross,
O my heart?
there is no traveller before you,
there is no road:
Where is the movement,
where is the rest,
on that shore?

There is no water; no boat, no boatman, is there;

There is not so much as a rope to tow the boat, nor a man to draw it.
No earth, no sky, no time, no thing, is there: no shore, no ford!

There, there is neither body nor mind:
and where is the place that shall still the thirst of the soul?
You shall find naught in that emptiness.
Be strong, and enter into your own body:
for there your foothold is firm.
Consider it well,
O my heart!
go not elsewhere,
Kabîr says: 'Put all imaginations away,
and stand fast in that which you are.'

How Humble Is God
God is the tree in the forests that
allows itself to die and will not defend itself in front of those
with the ax, not wanting to cause them
shame.

And God is the earth that will allow itself to
be deformed by man's tools, but He cries; yes, God cries,
but only in front of His closest ones.

And a beautiful animal is being beaten to death,
but nothing can make God break His silence
to the masses
and say,

"Stop, please stop, why are you doing this
to Me? "

How humble is God?
Kabir wept
when I
knew.

The Swan Flies Away
The Swan Will Fly Away All Alone,
Spectacle of the World Will Be a Mere Fair
As the Leaf Falls from the Tree
Is Difficult to Find
Who Knows Where it Will Fall
Once it is Struck with a Gust Of Wind
When Life Span is Complete
Then Listening to Orders, Following Others, Will Be Over
The Messengers of Yama are Very Strong
It's an Entanglement with the Yama
Servant Kabir Praises the Attributes of the Lord
He Finds the Lord Soon
Guru Will Go According to His Doings
The Disciple According to His!

I Burst Into Laughter
I burst into laughter
whenever I hear
that the fish is thirsty in water.

Without the knowledge of Self
people just wander to Mathura or to Kashi
like the musk-deer unaware
of the scent in his navel,
goes on running forest to forest.

In water is the lotus plant
and the plant bears flowers
and on the flowers are the bees buzzing.
Likewise all yogis and mendicants
and all those who have renounced comforts,
are on here and hereafter and the nether world -
contemplating.

Friend, the Supreme Indestructible Being,
on whom thousands of sages meditate
and even Brahma, Vishnu and Mahesh,
really resides within one's self.

Though He is near, He appears far away -
and that is what makes one disturbed;
says Kabir, listen, O wise one,
by Guru alone is the confusion curbed.

What Kind Of God?

What kind of God would He be
if He did not hear the
bangles ring on
an ant's
wrist

as they move the earth
in their sweet
dance?

And what kind of God would He be
if a leaf's prayer was not as precious to creation
as the prayer His own son sang
from the glorious depth
of his soul –
for us.

And what kind of God would He be
if the vote of millions in this world could sway Him
to change the divine
law of
love

that speaks so clearly with compassion's elegant tongue,
saying, eternally saying:

all are forgiven – moreover, dears,
no one has ever been
guilty.

What
kind of God would He be
if He did not count the blinks
of your
eyes

and is in absolute awe of their movements?

What a God - what a God we
have.

I Have Attained The Eternal Bliss

I have attained the Eternal Bliss.
There is no time for sorrow or pain,
for now I enjoy singing His glory.

The tree of His pleasure has neither root, nor seed,
as revealed by the grace of the true Guru.

Now there is effulgence of a million suns,
my swan has dipped in the lake of His knowledge.

Says Kabir, listen, O wise brother,
Now comings and goings have come to an end.

I Have Been Thinking
I have been thinking...
I have been thinking of the difference between water
I have been thinkingI have been thinkingand the waves on it. Rising,
water's still water, falling back,
it is water, will you give me a hint
how to tell them apart?

Because someone has made up the word
'wave,' do I have to distinguish it
from water?

There is a Secret One inside us;
the planets in all the galaxies
pass through his hands like beads.

That is a string of beads one should look at with luminous eyes.

I Laugh When I Hear That The Fish In The Water Is Thirsty
I laugh when I hear that the fish in the water is thirsty

You don't grasp the fact that what is most alive of all
is inside your own house.
and so you walk from one holy city to the next with
a confused look!

Kabir will tell you the truth: go wherever you like,
to Calcutta or Tibet;
if you can't find where your soul is hidden,
for you the world will never be real!

When He Himself Reveals Himself
When he himself reveals himself,
Brahma brings into manifestation
That which can never be seen.

As the seed is in the plant,
as the shade is in the tree,
as the void is in the sky,
as infinite forms are in the void-

So from beyond the Infinite,
the Infinite comes;

and from the Infinite the finite extends.

The creature is in Brahma,
and Brahma is in the creature:
they are ever distinct,
yet ever united.

He Himself is the tree, the seed, and the germ.
He Himself is the flower, the fruit, and the shade.
He Himself is the sun, the light, and the lighted.
He Himself is Brahma, creature, and Maya.
He Himself is the manifold form, the infinite space;
He is the breath, the word, and the meaning.

He Himself is the limit and the limitless:
and beyond both the limited and the limitless is He,
the Pure Being.

He is the Immanent Mind in Brahma and in the creature.

The Supreme Soul is seen within the soul,
The Point is seen within the Supreme Soul,
And within the Point, the reflection is seen again.
Kabîr is blest because he has this supreme vision!

I Played Day And Night
I played day and night with my comrades,
and now I am greatly afraid.

So high is my Lord's palace,
my heart trembles to mount its stairs:
yet I must not be shy, if I would enjoy His love.

My heart must cleave to my Lover;
I must withdraw my veil,
and meet Him with all my body:

Mine eyes must perform the ceremony of the lamps of love.

Kabîr says: 'Listen to me, friend:
he understands who loves.
If you feel not love's longing for your Beloved One,
it is vain to adorn your body,
vain to put unguent on your eyelids.'

I Said To The Wanting-Creature Inside Me
I said to the wanting-creature inside me:
What is this river you want to cross?
There are no travelers on the river-road, and no road.
Do you see anyone moving about on that bank, or nesting?

There is no river at all, and no boat, and no boatman.
There is no tow rope either, and no one to pull it.
There is no ground, no sky, no time, no bank, no ford!

And there is no body, and no mind!
Do you believe there is some place that will make the
soul less thirsty?
In that great absence you will find nothing.

Be strong then, and enter into your own body;
there you have a solid place for your feet.
Think about it carefully!
Don't go off somewhere else!

Kabir says this: just throw away all thoughts of
imaginary things,
and stand firm in that which you are.

When I Found The Boundless Knowledge
Kabir:
My mind was soothed
When I found the boundless knowledge,
And the fires
that scorch the world
To me are water cool.

I Talk To My Inner Lover, And I Say, Why Such Rush?
I talk to my inner lover, and I say, why such rush?
We sense that there is some sort of spirit that loves
birds and animals and the ants—
perhaps the same one who gave a radiance to you
in your mother's womb.
Is it logical you would be walking around entirely
orphaned now?
The truth is you turned away yourself,
and decided to go into the dark alone.
Now you are tangled up in others, and have forgotten
what you once knew,
and that's why everything you do has some weird
failure in it.

I Won't Come
I won't come
I won't go
I won't live
I won't die

I'll keep uttering

The name
And lose myself
In it

I'm bowl
And I'm platter
I'm man
And I'm woman

I'm grapefruit
And I'm sweet lime
I'm Hindu
And I'm Muslim

I'm fish
And I'm net
I'm fisherman
And I'm time

I'm nothing
Says Kabir
I'm not among the living
Or the dead.

When The Day Came
When the Day came -
The Day I had lived and died for -
The Day that is not in any calendar -
Clouds heavy with love
Showered me with wild abundance.
Inside me, my soul was drenched.
Around me, even the desert grew green.

Illusion And Reality
What is seen is not the Truth
What is cannot be said
Trust comes not without seeing
Nor understanding without words
The wise comprehends with knowledge
To the ignorant it is but a wonder
Some worship the formless God
Some worship His various forms
In what way He is beyond these attributes
Only the Knower knows
That music cannot be written
How can then be the notes
Says Kabir, awareness alone will overcome illusion

It Is Needless To Ask Of A Saint

It is needless to ask of a saint the caste to which he belongs;
For the priest, the warrior. the tradesman, and all the
thirty-six castes, alike are seeking for God.
It is but folly to ask what the caste of a saint may be;
The barber has sought God, the washerwoman, and the carpenter-
Even Raidas was a seeker after God.
The Rishi Swapacha was a tanner by caste.
Hindus and Moslems alike have achieved that End,
where remains no mark of distinction.

I've Burned My Own House Down
I've burned my own house down,
the torch is in my hand.
Now I'll burn down the house of anyone
who wants to follow me.

Knowing Nothing Shuts The Iron Gates
Knowing nothing shuts the iron gates;
the new love opens them.

The sound of the gates opening wakes
the beautiful woman asleep.

Kabir says: Fantastic!
Don't let a chance like this go by!

Lamps Burn In Every House
Lamps burn in every house,
O blind one! and you cannot see them.
One day your eyes shall suddenly be opened,
and you shall see: and the fetters of death will fall from you.
There is nothing to say or to hear,
there is nothing to do:
it is he who is living, yet dead, who shall never die again.

Because he lives in solitude,
therefore the Yogi says that his home is far away.

Your Lord is near: yet you are climbing the palm-tree to seek Him.

The Brahman priest goes from house to house
and initiates people into faith:
Alas! the true fountain of life is beside you,
and you have set up a stone to worship.

Kabîr says: 'I may never express how sweet my Lord is.
Yoga and the telling of beads,
virtue and vice-these are naught to Him.'

Lift The Veil

Lift the veil
that obscures
the heart

and there
you will find
what you are
looking for

Looking At The Grinding Stones - Dohas (Couplets) I

Looking at the grinding stones, Kabir laments
In the duel of wheels, nothing stays intact.

searching for the wicked, met not a single one
When searched myself, 'I' found the wicked one

Tomorrows work do today, today's work anon
if the moment is lost, when will the work be done

Speak such words, sans ego's ploy
Body remains composed, giving the listener joy

Slowly slowly O mind, everything in own pace happens
Gardner may water a hundred buckets, fruit arrives only in its season

Give so much O God, suffice to envelop my clan
I should not suffer cravings, nor the visitor goes unfed

In vain is the eminence, just like a date tree
No shade for travelers, fruit is hard to reach

Like seed contains the oil, fire in flint stone
Your heart seats the Divine, realize if you can

Kabira in the market place, wishes welfare of all
Neither friendship nor enmity with anyone at all

Reading books everyone died, none became any wise
One who reads the words of Love, only becomes wise

In anguish everyone prays to Him, in joy does none
To One who prays in happiness, how sorrow can come

When You Were Born In This world - Dohas II

When you were born in this world
Everyone laughed while you cried
Conduct not yourself in manner such
That they laugh when you are gone

Kabir's mind got cleansed like the holy Ganges water
Now everyone follows, saying Kabir Kabir

Guru the washer man, disciple is the cloth
The name of God liken to the soap
Wash the mind on foundation firm
To realize the glow of Truth

Alive one sees, alive one knows
Thus crave for salvation when full of life
Alive you did not cut the noose of binding actions
Hoping liberation with death!

Inexpressible is the story of Love
It cannot be revealed by words
Like the dumb eating sweet-meat
Only smiles, the sweetness he cannot tell

Worry is the bandit that eats into one's heart
What the doctor can do, what remedy to impart?

Says Kabir
Don't be so proud and vain
Looking at your high mansion
Death makes one lie on bare land
And grass will grow thereon

Says Kabir
Don't be so proud and vain
The clutches of Time are dark
Who knows where shall it kill
Whether at home or abroad

Says Kabir
By my doing nothing happens
What I don't does come to pass
If anything happens as if my doing
Then truly it is done by someone else

Like the pupil in the eyes
The Lord resides inside
Ignorant do not know this fact
They search Him outside

First the pangs of separation
Next grows the thirst for Love
Says Kabir then only hope
The union to materialize

Where Do You Search Me

Where do you search me?
I am with you
Not in pilgrimage, nor in icons
Neither in solitudes
Not in temples, nor in mosques
Neither in Kaba nor in Kailash
I am with you O man
I am with you
Not in prayers, nor in meditation
Neither in fasting
Not in yogic exercises
Neither in renunciation
Neither in the vital force nor in the body
Not even in the ethereal space
Neither in the womb of Nature
Not in the breath of the breath
Seek earnestly and discover
In but a moment of search
Says Kabir, Listen with care
Where your faith is, I am there.

Many Hoped
Many hoped
but no one found
Hari's heart.
Where do the senses rest?
Where do the Ram-chanters go?
Where do the bright ones go?
Corpses: all gone
to the same place.
Drunk on the juice
of Ram's bliss,
Kabir says,
I've said and I've said,
I'm tired of saying.

My Body And My mind
My body and my mind...

My body and my mind are in depression because
You are not with me.

How much I love you and want you in my house!
When I hear people describe me as your bride I look sideways ashamed,
because I know that far inside us we have never met.

Then what is this love of mine?

I don't really care about food, I don't really care about sleep,
I am restless indoors and outdoors.

The bride wants her lover as much as a thirsty man wants water.

And how will I find someone who will take a message
to the Guest from me?
How restless Kabir is all the time!
How much he wants to see the Guest!

My Body Is Flooded

My body is flooded
With the flame of Love.
My soul lives in
A furnace of bliss.

Love's fragrance
Fills my mouth,
And fans through all things
With each outbreath.

Where Spring, The Lord Of The Seasons

Where Spring, the lord of the seasons, reigneth,
there the Unstruck Music sounds of itself,
There the streams of light flow in all directions;
Few are the men who can cross to that shore!

There, where millions of Krishnas stand with hands folded,
Where millions of Vishnus bow their heads,
Where millions of Brahmas are reading the Vedas,
Where millions of Shivas are lost in contemplation,
Where millions of Indras dwell in the sky,
Where the demi-gods and the munis are unnumbered,
Where millions of Saraswatis, Goddess of Music, play on the veena
There is my Lord self-revealed:
and the scent of sandal and flowers dwells in those deeps.

My Swan, Let Us Fly

My swan, let us fly to that land
Where your Beloved lives forever.

That land has an up-ended well
Whose mouth, narrow as a thread,
The married soul draws water from
Without a rope or pitcher.

My swan, let us fly to that land
Where your Beloved lives forever.

Clouds never cluster there,
Yet it goes on and on raining.
Don't keep squatting outside in the yard –

Come in! Get drenched without a body!

My swan, let us fly to that land
Where your Beloved lives forever.

That land is always soaked in moonlight;
Darkness can never come near it.
It is flooded always with the dazzle
Of not one, but a million suns.

My swan, let us fly to that land
Where your Beloved lives forever.

O Friend

O friend! hope for Him whilst you live
O friend! hope for Him whilst you live,
know whilst you live, understand whilst you live:
for in life deliverance abides.

If your bonds be not broken whilst living,
what hope of deliverance in death?

It is but an empty dream, that the soul shall have union with Him
because it has passed from the body:

If He is found now, He is found then,
If not, we do but go to dwell in the City of Death.

If you have union now, you shall have it hereafter.

Bathe in the truth, know the true Guru,
have faith in the true Name!

Kabir says : 'It is the spirit of the quest which helps;
I am the slave of this Spirit of the quest.'

O How May I Ever Express That Secret Word?

O How may I ever express that secret word?
O how can I say He is not like this, and He is like that?
If I say that He is within me, the universe is ashamed:
If I say that He is without me, it is falsehood.
He makes the inner and the outer worlds to be indivisibly one;
The conscious and the unconscious, both are His footstools.
He is neither manifest nor hidden,
He is neither revealed nor unrevealed:
There are no words to tell that which He is.

O Lord Increate, Who Will Serve Thee?

O lord Increate, who will serve Thee?
Every votary offers his worship to the God of his own creation:
each day he receives service-
None seek Him, the Perfect:
Brahma, the Indivisible Lord.
They believe in ten Avatars;
but no Avatar can be the Infinite Spirit,
for he suffers the results of his deeds:
The Supreme One must be other than this.

The Yogi, the Sanyasi,
the Ascetics, are disputing one with another:

Kabîr says, 'O brother! he who has seen that radiance of love,
he is saved.'

O My Heart! The Supreme Spirit
O my heart!
the Supreme Spirit,
the great Master,
is near you: wake, oh wake!
Run to the feet of your Beloved:
for your Lord stands near to your head.
You have slept for unnumbered ages;
this morning will you not wake?

O Servant Where Dost Thou Seek Me
O servant, where dost thou seek Me?
O servant, where dost thou seek Me?

Lo! I am beside thee.

I am neither in temple nor in mosque:
I am neither in Kaaba nor in Kailash:

Neither am I in rites and ceremonies,
nor in Yoga and renunciation.

If thou art a true seeker, thou shalt at once see Me:
thou shalt meet Me in a moment of time.

Kabir says, ' O Sadhu! God is the breath of all breath.'

O Slave, Liberate Yourself
O Slave, liberate yourself.

Where are you, and where's your home,
find it in your lifetime, man.

If you fail to wake up now,
you'll be helpless when the end comes.

Says Kabir, listen, O wise one,

Oh Friend, I Love You, Think This Over
Oh friend, I love you, think this over
carefully! If you are in love,
then why are you asleep?

If you have found him,
give yourself to him, take him.

Why do you lose track of him again and again?

If you are about to fall into heavy sleep anyway,
why waste time smoothing the bed
and arranging the pillows?

Kabir will tell you the truth: this is what love is like:
suppose you had to cut your head off
and give it to someone else,
what difference would that make?

Plucking Your Eyebrows
Plucking your eyebrows,
Putting on mascara,
But will that help you
To see things anew?

The one who sees
Is changed into
The one who's seen
Only if one is

Salt and the other
Water. But you, says Kabir,
Are a dead
Lump of quartz.

Tell Me Brother
Tell me, Brother, how can I renounce Maya?
When I gave up the tying of ribbons, still I tied my garment about me:
When I gave up tying my garment, still I covered my body in its folds.
So, when I give up passion, I see that anger remains;
And when I renounce anger, greed is with me still;
And when greed is vanquished, pride and vainglory remain;
When the mind is detached and casts Maya away, still it clings to the letter.
Kabîr says, 'Listen to me, dear Sadhu! the true path is rarely found.'

Tell Me, O Swan, Your Ancient Tale
Tell me, O Swan, your ancient tale.
From what land do you come,
O Swan? to what shore will you fly?
Where would you take your rest,
O Swan, and what do you seek?

Even this morning, O Swan, awake, arise, follow me!
There is a land where no doubt nor sorrow have rule:
where the terror of Death is no more.
There the woods of spring are a-bloom,
and the fragrant scent 'He is I' is borne on the wind:
There the bee of the heart is deeply immersed,
and desires no other joy.

Tentacles Of Time
Oh Sadhu This is the Village of the Dead

The Saints Have Died, The God-Messengers Die
The Life-Filled Yogis Die Too
The Kings Die, The Subjects Die
The Healers and the Sick Die Too

The Moon Dies, The Sun Dies
The Earth and Sky Die Too
Even the Caretakers of the Fourteen Worlds Die
Why Hope For Any of These

The Nine Die, The Ten Die
The Eighty Eight Die Easily Too
The Thirty Three Crore Devatas Die
It's a Big Game of Time

The Un-Named Naam Lives Without Any End
There is No Other Truth
Says Kabir Listen Oh Sadhu
Don't Get Lost and Die

The Bhakti Path
The bhakti path winds in a delicate way.
On this path there is no asking and no not asking.
The ego simply disappears the moment you touch him.
The joy of looking for him is so immense that you just dive in,
and coast around like a fish in the water.
If anyone needs a head, the lover leaps up to offer his.

The Bride-Soul
When will that day dawn, Mother;
When the One I took birth for
Holds me to His heart with deathless love?
I long for the bliss of divine union.
I long to lose my body, mind, and soul
And become one with my husband.
When will that day dawn, Mother?
Husband, fulfil now the longing I have had
Since before the universe was made.
Enter me completely and release me.
In terrible lonely years without You
I yearn and yearn for You.
I spend sleepless nights hunting for You,
Gazing into darkness after You,
With unblinking hopeless eyes.
When will that day dawn, Mother?
When will my Lord hold me to His heart?
My empty bed, like a hungry tigress,
Devours me whenever I try to sleep.
Listen to your slave's prayer -
Come and put out this blaze of agony
That consumes my soul and body.
When will He hold me to His heart?
When will that day dawn, Mother?
Kabir sings, "If I ever meet You, my Beloved,
I'll cling to you so fiercely You melt into me;
I'll sing from inside You songs of union,
World-dissolving songs of Eternal Bliss."

The Dropp And The Sea
I went looking for Him
And lost myself;
The dropp merged with the Sea -
Who can find it now?

Looking and looking for Him
I lost myself;
The Sea merged with the dropp -
Who can find it now?

The Guest Is Inside You, And Also Inside Me
The Guest is inside you, and also inside me;
you know the sprout is hidden inside the seed.
We are all struggling; none of us has gone far.
Let your arrogance go, and look around inside.

The blue sky opens out further and farther,

the daily sense of failure goes away,
the damage I have done to myself fades,
a million suns come forward with light,
when I sit firmly in that world.

I hear bells ringing that no one has shaken,
inside 'love' there is more joy than we know of,
rain pours down, although the sky is clear of clouds,
there are whole rivers of light.
The universe is shot through in all parts by a single sort of love.
How hard it is to feel that joy in all our four bodies!

Those who hope to be reasonable about it fail.
The arrogance of reason has separated us from that love.
With the word 'reason' you already feel miles away.

How lucky Kabir is, that surrounded by all this joy
he sings inside his own little boat.
His poems amount to one soul meeting another.
These songs are about forgetting dying and loss.
They rise above both coming in and going out.

The Impossible Pass
The pundits have taken
A highway that takes them
away,
and they're gone.
Kabir has climbed to
The impossible pass
of Ram
and stayed.

The Last Flight
The Swan Will Fly Away All Alone,
Spectacle of the World Will Be a Mere Fair
As the Leaf Falls from the Tree
Is Difficult to Find
Who Knows Where it Will Fall
Once it is Struck with a Gust Of Wind
When Life Span is Complete
Then Listening to Orders, Following Others, Will Be Over
The Messengers of Yama are Very Strong
It's an Entanglement with the Yama
Servant Kabir Praises the Attributes of the Lord
He Finds the Lord Soon
Guru Will Go According to His Doings
The Disciple According to His

The Light Of The Sun

The light of the sun, the moon,
and the stars shines bright:
The melody of love swells forth,
and the rhythm of love's detachment beats the time.

Day and night, the chorus of music fills the heavens;
and Kabîr says 'My Beloved One gleams like the lightning flash in the sky.'

Do you know how the moments perform their adoration?
Waving its row of lamps,
the universe sings in worship day and night,
There are the hidden banner and the secret canopy:
There the sound of the unseen bells is heard.

Kabîr says: 'There adoration never ceases;
there the Lord of the Universe sitteth on His throne.'

The whole world does its works and commits its errors:
but few are the lovers who know the Beloved.

The devout seeker is he who mingles in his heart
the double currents of love and detachment,
like the mingling of the streams of Ganges and Jumna;
In his heart the sacred water flows day and night;
and thus the round of births and deaths is brought to an end.

Behold what wonderful rest is in the Supreme Spirit!
and he enjoys it, who makes himself meet for it.

Held by the cords of love,
the swing of the Ocean of Joy sways to and fro;
and a mighty sound breaks forth in song.

See what a lotus blooms there without water!
and Kabîr says 'My heart's bee drinks its nectar.'

What a wonderful lotus it is,
that blooms at the heart of the spinning wheel of the universe!
Only a few pure souls know of its true delight.
Music is all around it,
and there the heart partakes of the joy of the Infinite Sea.

Kabîr says: 'Dive thou into that Ocean of sweetness:
thus let all errors of life and of death flee away.'

Behold how the thirst of the five senses is quenched there!
and the three forms of misery are no more!

Kabîr says: 'It is the sport of the Unattainable One:
look within, and behold how the moon-beams
of that Hidden One shine in you.'

There falls the rhythmic beat of life and death:
Rapture wells forth, and all space is radiant with light.
There the Unstruck Music is sounded;
it is the music of the love of the three worlds.

There millions of lamps of sun and of moon are burning;
There the drum beats, and the lover swings in play.
There love-songs resound, and light rains in showers;
and the worshipper is entranced in the taste of the heavenly nectar.
Look upon life and death; there is no separation between them,
The right hand and the left hand are one and the same.
Kabîr says: 'There the wise man is speechless;
for this truth may never be found in Vadas or in books.'

I have had my Seat on the Self-poised One,
I have drunk of the Cup of the Ineffable,
I have found the Key of the Mystery,
I have reached the Root of Union.
Travelling by no track,
I have come to the Sorrowless Land:
very easily has the mercy of the great Lord come upon me.

They have sung of Him as infinite and unattainable:
but I in my meditations have seen Him without sight.
That is indeed the sorrowless land,
and none know the path that leads there:
Only he who is on that path has surely transcended all sorrow.

Wonderful is that land of rest,
to which no merit can win;
It is the wise who has seen it,
it is the wise who has sung of it.
This is the Ultimate Word:
but can any express its marvellous savour?
He who has savoured it once,
he knows what joy it can give.

Kabîr says: 'Knowing it,
the ignorant man becomes wise,
and the wise man becomes speechless and silent,
The worshipper is utterly inebriated,
His wisdom and his detachment are made perfect;
He drinks from the cup of the inbreathings and the outbreathings of love.'

There the whole sky is filled with sound,
and there that music is made without fingers and without strings;
There the game of pleasure and pain does not cease.
Kabîr says: 'If you merge your life in the Ocean of Life,
you will find your life in the Supreme Land of Bliss.'

What a frenzy of ecstasy there is in every hour!
and the worshipper is pressing out and drinking the essence of the hours:

he lives in the life of Brahma.

I speak truth, for I have accepted truth in life;
I am now attached to truth,
I have swept all tinsel away.

Kabîr says: 'Thus is the worshipper set free from fear;
thus have all errors of life and of death left him.'

There the sky is filled with music:
There it rains nectar:
There the harp-strings jingle,
and there the drums beat.
What a secret splendour is there,
in the mansion of the sky!
There no mention is made of the rising and the setting of the sun;

In the ocean of manifestation,
which is the light of love,
day and night are felt to be one.

Joy for ever, no sorrow,-no struggle!
There have I seen joy filled to the brim, perfection of joy;
No place for error is there.
Kabîr says: 'There have I witnessed the sport of One Bliss! '

I have known in my body the sport of the universe:
I have escaped from the error of this world..
The inward and the outward are become as one sky,
the Infinite and the finite are united:
I am drunken with the sight of this All!
This Light of Thine fulfils the universe:
the lamp of love that burns on the salver of knowledge.
Kabîr says: 'There error cannot enter,
and the conflict of life and death is felt no more.'

Within This Earthen Vessel
Within this earthen vessel are bowers and groves,
and within it is the Creator:
Within this vessel are the seven oceans
and the unnumbered stars.
The touchstone and the jewel-appraiser are within;
and within this vessel the Eternal soundeth,
and the spring wells up.
Kabîr says:
'Listen to me, my Friend!
My beloved Lord is within.'

www.ingramcontent.com/pod-product-compliance
Lightning Source LLC
Chambersburg PA
CBHW061314040426
42444CB00010B/2642